HOW TO M

SELL MILK BATH FOR

BEGINNERS

Step-By-Step Guide To Craft, Market, And Sell Organic Products Successfully

REMINGTON BRIGGS

DISCLAIMER

Greetings from the world of crafts! Before exploring the fascinating realm of creativity and craftsmanship that this book presents, we would like to make sure that the content is understood and can be clearly understood. This book's contents are meant solely for informational purposes. Although every attempt has been taken to guarantee accuracy and dependability, the material provided should not be used in place of or as a substitute for expert advice. Since every person's path with creating is different, we advise readers to use good judgment and, if necessary, seek out qualified professional guidance.

Crafting calls for imagination, trial & error, and individual interpretation. As a result, depending on personal abilities, tools utilized, and methods employed, outcomes may differ. The concepts, methods, or recommendations offered in this book are not guaranteed to produce any particular results, nor do the writers and publishers of the book. Additionally, it's critical to take safety precautions when working on crafts. Prioritize your own safety and well-being, use the proper tools and equipment, and always adhere to the manufacturer's recommendations.

We urge readers to be aware of their strengths and weaknesses and to experiment, be creative, and enjoy the making process.

TABLE OF CONTENTS

ABOUT THE BOOK

For anyone interested in the craft of creating opulent milk baths, the book "How to Make and Sell Milk Bath" is a must-have resource. It explores the essential elements of milk baths, beginning with an overview that clarifies what milk baths are and the reasons behind their growing popularity in beauty regimens. It's important to know the advantages of milk baths, and this book goes into great detail about how they can hydrate skin, reduce irritation, promote anti-aging, and induce a spa-like sense of relaxation and stress relief.

The book goes into great detail about the necessary supplies, ingredients, and safety measures to get you started with milk baths. To guarantee a seamless and pleasurable experience for both novices and seasoned aficionados, frequently asked questions and concerns are addressed.

The content of the book is divided into chapters that address the fundamentals of milk baths, such as their history, the kinds of milk that are used, extra components like honey and essential oils, mixing methods, and advice on how to store and preserve freshness over time. The advantages of skincare and health are thoroughly examined, and dermatologists' opinions provide a qualified viewpoint.

The best part about DIY milk bath recipes is that they give readers a variety of options, from simple formulas to scented versions, herbal infusions, and specialist milk baths catered to particular skin types. Innovative packaging concepts are also exchanged to assist business owners in making their goods aesthetically pleasing and ready for the market.

Understanding the necessary equipment, hygienic procedures, ingredient arrangement, workspace security, and time-saving strategies are all important when setting up a workplace for making milk baths. These elements are essential for effectiveness and high-quality output.

The identification of target audiences, branding, price strategies, online and offline sales channels, and customer engagement tactics to foster enduring connections and loyalty are all included under the umbrella of marketing and selling strategies.

To guarantee adherence to FDA requirements, ingredient transparency, liability insurance, quality control procedures, and competent handling of customer complaints, legal and regulatory factors are taken into account.

Expanding production, outsourcing choices, employing support, inventory control, and financial planning are all part of scaling a milk bath company for long-term success and profitability. It is essential to use customer feedback and improvement tactics to improve products, encourage ongoing innovation, and effectively address criticism.

To fulfill changing market demands and maintain competitiveness, expanding product lines and offerings is encouraged through product diversification, seasonal variations, collaborations, customization services, and sustainability initiatives.

The book also looks at potential future developments in the milk bath sector, such as keeping abreast of market shifts, entering new markets, and utilizing technology to advance a company's operations, launching training programs, and developing international expansion plans.

"How to Make and Sell Milk Bath" is a thorough manual that not only teaches the technique of creating beautiful milk baths but also gives entrepreneurs the tools they need to create profitable companies in this niche market, interact with clients, and grow their brands to new heights.

CHAPTER ONE

MILK BATH OVERVIEW

KNOWING WHAT A MILK BATH IS AND WHY IT'S SO POPULAR

From ancient civilizations like Egypt and Greece, milk baths have been utilized for ages as opulent skincare treatments. They include taking a milk-and-other-nourishing-ingredient-infused bath. The popularity of milk baths can be attributed to their capacity to soften and moisturize skin while offering a luxurious and calming experience.

The advantages of milk baths for skin care are among the main reasons they're so popular. Lactic acid, a natural exfoliator found in milk, aids in removing dead skin cells to reveal smoother, more radiant skin. Furthermore, milk's proteins and fats nourish and moisturize the skin, giving it a more youthful, radiant appearance. Because they hydrate and exfoliate the skin, milk baths are a great option for anyone trying to improve the general health and appearance of their skin.

MILK BATH BENEFITS: EXAMINING ITS ADVANTAGES FOR SKINCARE

Milk baths are good for more than just softening and moisturizing the skin. They are especially helpful for people with dry or sensitive skin issues because they can also aid in reducing inflammation and irritation.

Milk's lactic acid functions as a mild exfoliator, encouraging cell renewal and diminishing the visibility of wrinkles and fine lines.

To address certain skincare issues, milk baths can also be tailored with extra components like oatmeal, honey, or essential oils.

For instance, oats help reduce inflammation and itching, while lavender essential oil might improve relaxation and encourage better sleep. Because of their adaptability, milk baths can be used as an efficient skincare treatment for a variety of skin types.

STARTING: NECESSARY SUPPLIES AND EQUIPMENT

To make a milk bath at home, there are a few necessary supplies and equipment. First, pick a bathtub or washbasin that is big enough for you to bathe in comfortably.

Next, gather your ingredients: milk (for richness, use powdered or full-fat milk), optional additions (such as honey or essential oils), and a spoon or whisk for mixing.

Pour warm water into your bathtub and add as much milk and other ingredients as you like.

To uniformly spread the ingredients throughout the water, use your mixing instrument. Just soak and unwind in the bath for 15 to 30 minutes, letting the milk and other ingredients do their magic on your skin.

SAFETY MEASURES: GUARANTEEING A JOYFUL AND SAFE EXPERIENCE

Even though milk baths are usually soothing and harmless for the skin, there are a few things you need to know to make sure you have a good experience. To start, make sure the water is not too hot or uncomfortable. Not too hot, but just warm enough to open pores and ease tense muscles.

Furthermore, it's advisable to stay away from milk baths or use suitable substitutes if you have any known allergies or sensitivities to dairy products. To prevent any allergic reactions, always test new ingredients on a tiny area of skin before using them in a whole bath.

FAQS AND COMMON QUESTIONS: CLEARING UP MISUNDERSTANDINGS AND UNCERTAINTIES

The majority of skin types can benefit from milk baths, but individuals who have severe allergies, sensitivities, or lactose intolerance should exercise caution or use other components. Additionally, it's critical to remember that milk baths should only be used as a supplement to a thorough skincare regimen and should never be used in place of medical treatments for skin disorders.

How frequently one can have a milk bath is another subject that comes up a lot. Individual tastes and skin demands determine how often a person should have a milk bath.

Weekly milk baths could be beneficial for some people, but they might be better enjoyed as a special treat for others. For optimal effects, pay attention to your skin's needs and modify your bathing regimen accordingly.

CHAPTER TWO

THE FUNDAMENTALS OF MILK BATHING

THE HISTORY AND ORIGINS OF MILK BATHS: A TRACE OF THEIR HISTORY

Milk baths have a long history that dates back hundreds of years to the time when milk was prized for its ability to nurture the skin by ancient civilizations like the Greeks and Egyptians. Famous for her beauty, Cleopatra was known to take opulent milk baths because she thought it kept her skin glowing and young. Milk baths were particularly well-liked by royalty and the upper class and were connected with beauty rituals in many civilizations.

Due to their moisturizing and exfoliating properties, milk baths have become a popular spa and self-care ritual in modern times.

These days, milk baths are a useful method for organically nourishing and revitalizing the skin in addition to being a symbol of luxury. Knowing the background of milk baths gives them more allure and links us to age-old beauty secrets that still influence wellness practices across the globe.

MILK TYPES USED: GOAT MILK, COW MILK, AND SUBSTITUTES

The kind of milk used to make milk baths is important since it affects the bath's qualities and advantages. Because of its high-fat content, cow's milk softens and moisturizes the skin beautifully. Conversely, goat's milk is perfect for sensitive skin types because of its special combination of vitamins and proteins that provide nourishing and calming effects.

Almond milk and coconut milk are examples of plant-based milk that can be used by anyone looking for vegan or alternative solutions. These substitutes offer their unique blend of skin-beneficial ingredients to the bath in addition to catering to those with dairy sensitivities.

You can tailor your experience with a milk bath to the requirements and preferences of your skin by experimenting with different kinds of milk.

EXTRA INGREDIENTS INCLUDE HERBS, ESSENTIAL OILS, AND HONEY.

Honey, essential oils, and herbs are examples of complementing items that can be added to a milk bath to increase its effects. Renowned for its antibacterial and moisturizing qualities, honey helps seal in moisture and encourages a radiant complexion. For their aroma therapeutic properties, essential oils like eucalyptus, lavender, or chamomile can be added to the bath to help with stress relief and relaxation.

Adding herbs to the bathwater, such as calendula, mint, or rose petals, not only gives it a luxurious touch but also enriches it with nutrients and antioxidants that are good for the skin. These extra ingredients create a spa-like experience in the comfort of your own home, enhancing not only the sensory pleasure of a milk bath but also its general skin-nourishing effects.

MIXING TECHNIQUES: COMBINING COMPONENTS TO ACHIEVE THE BEST OUTCOMES

The secret to a good milk bath knows just how to mix components to get the best possible outcome. To begin, slowly pour the necessary amount of milk into warm bathwater, making sure to spread it evenly. Then add more ingredients, such as honey, herbs, and essential oils, and whisk everything together gently to combine it all.

Steer clear of boiling water since this can reduce the substances' healthful qualities. Rather, use warm water to preserve the strength of the milk and other ingredients. Before stepping into the opulent bath, let the ingredients a few minutes to infuse into the water. This will guarantee a restorative and calming experience from beginning to end.

KEEPING FRESHNESS AND POTENCY INTACT DURING STORAGE AND SHELF LIFE

Appropriate storage is key to maintaining the efficacy and freshness of your homemade milk bath solutions. Any leftovers should be kept in sealed containers out of the direct sun and dampness, as these elements can eventually deteriorate if exposed to light and moisture.

To keep track of the containers' shelf life, label them with the preparation date.

Use your homemade milk bath mixes within a few weeks of preparation for the best results and to guarantee that all of their advantages are retained. It is recommended to reject the mixture and make a new batch if you observe any changes in the mixture's color, texture, or aroma. You can benefit from the nutritious advantages of your milk baths whenever you need a little self-care by according to these storage rules.

CHAPTER THREE

ADVANTAGES FOR SKINCARE AND HEALTH

MILK BATHS' MOISTURISING EFFECTS: HOW THEY HYDRATE THE SKIN

Because of their great moisturizing qualities, milk baths are a recommended treatment for dry, parched skin. The secret is in the natural fats and proteins found in milk, especially in whole milk or cream, which creates a barrier that keeps moisture in and prevents the skin from losing water.

These nutrients seep into the skin during a milk bath, leaving it feeling smooth, supple, and intensely hydrated. This is especially advantageous for people with sensitive or dry skin types because it hydrates the skin for an extended period without requiring thick creams or lotions.

First, add warm water to your bathtub to produce a moisturizing milk bath. Pour in a large measure of whole milk or powdered milk into the water and mix until well dissolved. Adding a few drops of essential oils, such as lavender or chamomile, which are well-known for their calming and hydrating qualities, can also improve the moisturizing effects. When the bath is ready, get in and let the milk do its job for a good fifteen to twenty minutes. After that, gently pat your skin dry to preserve the moisturizing effects.

RELIEVING ITCHING: RELAXING IMPACTS ON SENSITIVE SKIN

A calming remedy for sensitive or inflammatory skin disorders, milk baths are known for their extraordinary ability to relieve discomfort. Lactalbumin and lactoglobulin, two milk proteins, have anti-inflammatory qualities that can lessen redness, itching, and discomfort. Furthermore, milk's mild pH balances the skin's natural acidity, lowering the possibility of additional irritation or dryness. This makes milk baths a mildly beneficial choice for people with dermatitis, eczema, or other sensitive skin conditions.

Fill your bathtub with lukewarm water (not too hot, as heat can aggravate inflammation) to produce a calming milk bath for inflamed skin. After adding a cup of calming colloidal oatmeal to the water, add your preferred milk—goat's milk or whole milk, for example—to the mixture. To equally distribute the ingredients, give the mixture a good stir. Spend fifteen to twenty minutes soaking in the bath, allowing the calming effects of muesli and milk to ease pain and encourage skin repair. After that, pat your skin dry gently so as not to rub or irritate sensitive regions.

Benefits of Anti-Aging: Encouraging Youthful-Looking Skin

In addition to providing moisture and relaxation, milk baths include anti-aging properties that help skin retain its youthful appearance by enhancing its suppleness and texture. Over time, the lactic acid in milk can help minimize the appearance of fine lines and wrinkles by stimulating cell turnover and gently sloughing off dead skin cells. Furthermore, milk has antioxidants like vitamins A and E that support the development of collagen for firmer, more robust skin and shield the skin from environmental damage.

Incorporate a cup of powdered milk or several cups of whole milk into your warm bathwater to maximize the anti-aging benefits of this bath treatment.

Adding components like honey, which is well-known for being moisturizing and rich in antioxidants, can improve its anti-aging qualities. To make sure the components are dispersed equally throughout the water, thoroughly mix. Allow the milk and honey to nourish your skin and enhance its overall texture while you soak in the tub for 20 to 30 minutes. Over time, regular usage of milk baths can help to promote a more luminous and youthful complexion.

CREATING A SPA-LIKE EXPERIENCE FOR RELAXATION AND STRESS RELIEF

Beyond its advantages for skincare, taking a milk bath can provide you with a sumptuous, spa-like experience in the comfort of your own home, fostering calm and stress reduction. The calming effects of milk mixed with warm water help release stiff muscles, reducing physical tension and exhaustion. Furthermore, the subtle aroma of milk and any other essential oils may offer aroma therapeutic benefits that help to promote well-being and soothe the mind.

First, prepare your bathroom for relaxation by adding some soft lighting, soothing music, and even some candles for the atmosphere. This will help you have a peaceful milk bath. Pour some warm water into your bathtub and then add as much liquid or powdered milk as you like, swirling to make sure it's all equally distributed. Because essential oils have a relaxing and mood-enhancing impact, you may personalize the experience by adding a few drops of lavender, chamomile, or ylang-ylang essential oil. Spend at least 20 to 30 minutes soaking in the bathtub to help you relax and release tension.

To extend the benefits of your milk bath for relaxation, take your time patting dry and moisturizing your skin.

DERMATOLOGIST PERSPECTIVES: EXPERT VIEWS ON MILK BATHS

Dermatologists validate the effectiveness of milk's nutrients for skin care and provide insightful professional commentary on the advantages of milk baths.

They frequently draw attention to milk's moisturizing qualities, emphasizing how its ability to improve skin barrier function and provide moisture can help people with dry or sensitive skin disorders. Furthermore, milk has calming and anti-inflammatory properties that doctors highlight, which makes it a good choice for people with psoriasis, eczema, or other inflammatory skin conditions.

Dermatologists recognize that milk's lactic acid plays a part in stimulating cell turnover and gently exfoliating the skin, both of which can lead to a more youthful-looking complexion when it comes to anti-aging. They could advise milk baths as a component of an all-encompassing skincare regimen to keep skin looking young and healthy. Dermatologists also acknowledge that milk baths can help relax and relieve stress, emphasizing the need for self-care and mindfulness in enhancing general skin health and wellbeing.

Understanding the science behind milk baths' skincare advantages will help you make more informed decisions about including them in your routine for the best possible skin health and relaxation. This can be achieved by adding dermatological insights into your understanding of milk baths.

CHAPTER FOUR

HANDMADE MILK BATH RECIPES

SIMPLE RECIPE FOR MILK BATH

It's easier than you might think to make your milk bath at home. Gather your ingredients first. You may add optional extras like Epsom salts for added relaxation or powdered milk, such as whole milk or buttermilk powder. Make sure to thoroughly mix one cup of Epsom salts and two cups of powdered milk in a mixing dish. With each use, this base recipe gives your skin a nutritious bath that leaves it feeling moisturized and silky.

When the combination is prepared, put it in a tightly closed container to be used later. Just add a fair amount to warm bathwater and whisk to dissolve it to enjoy your milk bath. Give the milk and salts in the opulent mixture a minimum of 20 minutes to perform their magic on your skin by soaking in it. To maintain the moisturizing effects, rinse your skin with clean water and pat it dry gently.

AROMATIC SUBTYPES

Scents that stimulate your senses might be added to your milk bath to improve the experience. Popular options include essential oils with calming properties like chamomile or peppermint for a refreshing tingling or lavender for relaxation. Add a small amount of your preferred essential oil to the powdered milk and salt mixture, starting with a few drops. Remember that some oils are more intense than others, so adjust the aroma strength to your preferred level.

To keep the aroma of your fragrant milk bath mix fresh, wrap it in airtight containers after adding the scent. When you're ready to use it, go with the standard milk bath recipe and savor the extra sensory experience of your personalized aroma. In addition to improving your bath experience, this personalized touch helps your items stick out to prospective customers who are searching for unusual combinations.

HERBAL CONCOCTIONS

An at-home spa experience could be achieved by adding natural herbs to your milk bath mix. In addition to being aesthetically pleasing, herbs like chamomile flowers rose petals, and lavender buds also have medicinal uses.

To release the fragrant oils from your chosen herbs, start by crushing or grinding them. Add them to your base of powdered milk and salt, varying the quantity according to the advantages and scent you want.

Once blended, present your herbal-infused milk bath blend in eye-catching containers that highlight the vibrant herbs. Enjoy the relaxing effects of the herbal infusion by making use of the simple milk bath recipe. This inclusion appeals to people looking for holistic skincare solutions in addition to giving your product a more natural touch.

UNIQUE MILK BATHS

Add unique ingredients to your milk bath to tailor it to specific skin needs. Add cocoa powder for its antioxidant properties, coconut milk powder for added moisture, or colloidal oatmeal for relieving sensitive skin. Try out different combinations to make special mixes that address different skin issues.

To draw clients searching for specialized skincare products, emphasize the main advantages of each kind when promoting specialty milk baths. Give precise directions on how to use each combination to get the best outcomes possible, highlighting the nourishing qualities of the additional ingredients. You can serve a wide spectrum of clients who are looking for certain skincare benefits by offering a variety of specialty milk baths.

INNOVATIVE PACKAGING CONCEPTS

Your milk bath items will look better when they are packaged in unique ways that reflect the essence of your company. For a nostalgic touch, use glass jars with pretty labels, eco-friendly bags with vibrant patterns, or tins with a vintage feel. Utilize branding components such as colors, logos, and product descriptions to create a unified appearance that draws attention to products on shelves or online.

Make sure your milk bath items are tightly wrapped when packaging them to preserve freshness and shield them from moisture. To let clients know about the advantages of your creations, including ingredient lists, usage instructions, and any other pertinent product information. Interesting packaging helps increase brand recognition and repeat business in addition to improving the customer experience overall.

CHAPTER FIVE

ORGANIZING YOUR WORK AREA

OVERVIEW OF EQUIPMENT: MUST-HAVE ITEMS FOR MAKING A MILK BATH

Having the appropriate tools on hand can make a big difference when preparing a milk bath. Below is a list of all the necessary equipment. To properly integrate your ingredients, you will first need a large mixing basin or container. This dish needs to be substantial and roomy enough to comfortably fit the amounts called for in your recipe. Moreover, spend money on a whisk or spoon to ensure that your milk bath mix is thoroughly mixed and has a consistent consistency. A set of measuring spoons and cups is essential for precise ingredient measurements.

These will assist you in keeping the proper ratios for a well-rounded and potent product.

To remove any clumps or contaminants from the combination, a cheesecloth or fine mesh strainer is an additional essential item. For your milk bath to have a silky, opulent feel, this step is essential. Remember to include packaging supplies like jars or containers for presenting and keeping your final product. To maintain freshness and avoid infection, choose airtight containers. Finally, for a polished finish, think about spending money on labeling supplies like stickers or tags to prominently display the contents, usage guidelines, and branding information on your milk baths.

HYGIENE PRACTICES: UPHOLDING HYGIENIC CONDITIONS

To ensure the safety of the product and the happiness of the consumer, it is crucial to maintain high standards of cleanliness and sanitation in the production of milk baths. Firstly, wash your hands well with soap and water before touching any equipment or materials. To stop bacterial growth and cross-contamination, use sanitized dishes, containers, and utensils. To provide a clean environment for production, regularly use disinfectants to sanitize your workspace and surfaces.

To avoid getting contaminated, keep your hands away from your skin when handling chemicals. When measuring and mixing ingredients, especially when handling delicate or perishable substances, wear gloves or use appropriate utensils. To keep your components safe from moisture, dust, and vermin, stores them in airtight containers. To avoid accumulation and guarantee product integrity, keep your equipment and storage spaces clean regularly. Customers will be able to trust you to provide them with safe, high-quality milk baths if you put hygiene procedures first.

INGREDIENT ORGANISING: EFFECTIVE STORAGE STRATEGIES

Keeping your ingredients well-organized not only saves time but also guarantees lifespan and freshness. Assign names, dates of purchase, and expiration dates to every ingredient to ensure inventory is tracked and usage is prioritized according to freshness. To maintain their efficacy and aroma, dry components like as powdered milk, essential oils, and botanicals should be kept in sealed containers in a cool, dark environment. Use opaque or tinted bottles for liquid substances, such as carrier oils and extracts, to protect them from light exposure, which over time can deteriorate their quality.

Sort your materials into groups based on similarity to facilitate simple access when producing. To make replenishing easier and prevent running out of necessary ingredients in the middle of a recipe, keep a list of ingredients and their quantities. Investing in storage solutions such as cupboards, shelves, or storage bins can help you maintain a clutter-free and organized workstation. Keeping an orderly inventory of ingredients will help you produce milk bath products more efficiently, with less waste, and with consistently high quality.

WORKPLACE SAFETY: AVOIDING MISHAPS AND LEAKS

When preparing a milk bath, it is essential to ensure workplace safety to avoid spills and mishaps. To prevent breathing in small particles from powdered materials, keep your workspace well-ventilated. When working with concentrated essential oils, wear safety equipment such as gloves and goggles to avoid irritating your skin or eyes.

When not in use, keep your tools and equipment secure to avoid tripping hazards. To keep your workstation organized and secure, try not to fill it with extraneous objects. If spills occur, wipe them up right once to avoid trips and falls.

TIME-SAVING STRATEGIES: SIMPLIFYING YOUR MANUFACTURING PROCESS

Try batching related processes together to save time and streamline your milk bath production process. To cut down on preparation time for each session, measure the dry ingredients for many batches ahead of time.

Reduce the number of measuring and mixing processes by using pre-made mixes for typical blends.

To boost productivity and consistency in your milk bath goods, employ a set recipe and process to optimize your operation. Invest in equipment such as a timer to precisely record mixing and resting times and a digital scale for exact measures. To maximize production and find development opportunities, regularly assess and optimize your process.

CHAPTER SIX

STRATEGIES FOR MARKETING AND SELLING

IDENTIFICATION OF YOUR TARGET AUDIENCE: COMPREHENDING YOUR POSSIBLE CLIENTELE

The key to effectively marketing and selling milk baths is determining who your target market is. Investigate factors like age, gender, geography, and income level first. By using this data, you may better target your marketing efforts to the correct audiences.

For example, if your study indicates that young individuals in urban locations are drawn to self-care items, you might produce material emphasizing the relaxation and skincare benefits of milk baths to appeal to this group.

Take a closer look at psychographics after that to learn more about the values, interests, lifestyles, and problems of your target audience. To get insights, administer surveys, or interact with prospective clients on social media. For instance, you might discover that customers who care about the environment like skincare products with organic ingredients. Make use of this knowledge to draw in eco-aware customers by highlighting the sustainable and natural features of your milk bath products.

Finally, to further narrow down your target audience, study competition strategies and market trends. Determine the market gaps or USPs (unique selling points) that makes your milk baths stand out.

You can efficiently personalize your marketing communications to the preferences and demands of your potential clients, which will increase the likelihood of sales and customer satisfaction.

PRODUCT BRANDING: CRAFTING A DISTINCTIVE PERSONA FOR YOUR MILK BATHS

Building consumer loyalty and setting your milk baths apart from the competition both depend heavily on your branding. Establish the mission, values, and distinctive selling propositions of your brand before moving forward.

To appeal to customers who are concerned about their health and the environment, for instance, emphasize in your branding that your milk baths are created using organic components that are locally sourced.

Create a recognizable logo, color scheme, and packaging design that capture the essence of your business to create a unified visual identity. Brand identification and trust are strengthened when there is consistency across all touchpoints, including social media posts and product labeling. To draw in new clients and entice them to test your products, highlight the uses and advantages of your milk baths using eye-catching photography and a gripping narrative.

Make good use of digital channels to expand your audience and increase brand recognition. Provide interesting information like how-tos, client endorsements, and behind-the-scenes looks at your production workflow.

To increase your visibility and credibility, work with influencers or affiliate with other brands that complement yours.

Strong brand identities help you draw in devoted clients who are drawn to your products and principles.

PRICING STRATEGIES: ESTABLISHING PROFITABLE YET COMPETITIVE PRICES

Achieving the ideal price for your milk baths involves striking a balance between profitability and competition. Determine your production costs first, taking into account labor, ingredients, packaging, and overhead. Take into account the targeted profit margin as well as data from market research on the trends in product prices. While being competitive in the market, try to set your prices at a level that corresponds to the quality of your milk baths.

Providing many product options or package discounts might draw in a larger clientele and boost revenue. For repeat business, you may, for instance, make gift sets with matching skincare products or provide subscription services.

To modify pricing strategies, such as offering special discounts during holiday seasons or releasing limited-edition collections at premium rates, keep an eye on customer feedback and sales statistics.

Use dynamic pricing techniques in response to market conditions, seasonality, and rival activity. Track consumer preferences, price elasticity, and market trends with pricing analytics tools.

To maximize sales and keep a healthy profit margin, regularly assess and improve your pricing strategy. Customers' perceived value and willingness to buy are increased when you have clear pricing rules and use value-based messaging to support your rates.

SALES CHANNELS: INVESTIGATING LOCAL MARKETPLACES AND INTERNET PLATFORMS

Increasing the variety of your sales channels broadens your consumer base and makes you more approachable. Think about putting your milk baths up for sale on websites like your own, Amazon, Etsy, or other related marketplaces.

Enhance product listings to increase visibility and sales by adding relevant keywords, thorough descriptions, and high-quality photos.

Investigate forming alliances with nearby merchants, spas, boutiques, or farmers' markets to take advantage of offline sales opportunities and attract clients who enjoy in-person shopping. Provide rewards like discounts, special offers, or promotions to promote client loyalty and repeat business.

Promote your products with targeted advertising campaigns or increase traffic to your online store by utilizing social media and digital marketing tactics.

Utilize user-generated content, customer testimonials, and influencer partnerships to increase brand recognition and credibility, which will ultimately lead to an increase in sales across a variety of sales channels.

CUSTOMER INTERACTION: FOSTERING TIES AND ALLEGIANCE

Customer engagement is essential to creating enduring bonds and encouraging brand loyalty. To improve the total customer experience, put customer-centric initiatives into practice, such as customized communication, fast customer assistance, and loyalty programs.

To learn about the preferences, problems, and levels of satisfaction of your customers, gather and evaluate their feedback via surveys, reviews, and social media interactions. Utilize this information to enhance product offers, respond to consumer complaints, and modify marketing plans to better suit target audiences.

Provide interesting information that enhances the experiences of your customers and motivates them to engage with your brand, such as guides, advice, and user-generated material. Encourage a feeling of community by answering comments, holding freebies or competitions, and displaying client endorsements to establish credibility and social proof.

Maintain a relationship-building approach with current clients by sending out newsletters, follow-up emails, and exclusive deals to promote advocacy and recurring business. To increase your client base and boost sales, get satisfied consumers to tell others about their experiences and recommend your company to others. This is known as word-of-mouth marketing.

CHAPTER SEVEN

REGULATORY AND LEGAL ASPECTS

OBSERVANCE OF FDA GUIDELINES FOR PRODUCT LABELLING

It's critical to follow FDA requirements when it comes to the product labeling for your milk bath products. To protect consumer safety and product integrity, the FDA regulates cosmetics, which include bath products like milk baths. The identity of the product, the net quantity of its contents, a list of ingredients arranged in decreasing order of predominance, information about the maker or distributor, and any appropriate warnings or precautions must all be included on your labels.

Although comprehending these criteria can be intimidating for novices, it's crucial for both legal compliance and gaining the trust of customers. The FDA's requirements for cosmetic labeling are a good place to start because they are very specific and explain exactly what information has to be on the labels of your milk bath products. Make use of internet resources or regulatory experts' advice to make sure your labels fulfill all applicable regulations.

Producing labels that comply requires meticulous attention to precision and detail. Verify ingredient lists twice, make sure net quantity declarations are correct, and include any necessary cautions or warnings related to the substances in your product. You may increase client confidence in your milk bath products by exhibiting a dedication to quality and transparency by strictly adhering to FDA requirements.

INGREDIENT TRANSPARENCY: REVEALING INGREDIENTS TO BUILD CONSUMER CONFIDENCE

Gaining the trust of your customers requires being open and honest about the contents of your milk bath product. Because consumers are becoming more conscious of what they put on their skin, ingredient transparency is a key differentiator. Start by enumerating every element that went into your milk bath, including any additions or preservatives as well as basic constituents like milk powders and essential oils.

For novices, navigating ingredient transparency entails being aware of each component's function and possible effects on skin health. Look about the advantages of popular components used in milk baths, such as their ability to moisturize, their calming effects, or their potential for aromatherapy.

To inform customers, make sure that these advantages are spelled out on product labels and promotional materials.

In a competitive market, adding ingredient clarity to your marketing plan will help your milk bath products stand out. Draw attention to the natural and organic components in your product, highlight any certifications or quality standards your ingredients have met, and answer typical questions from customers about allergies and sensitivities. You gain credibility and trust from your target market by being honest about the ingredients in your products.

LIABILITY INSURANCE: GUARDING YOUR COMPANY AGAINST DANGERS

Getting liability insurance is essential to safeguarding your milk bath company from legal ramifications and hazards.

Insurance can protect you against monetary losses brought on by events involving your products, such as allergic reactions or property damage. For novices, being aware of the many insurance options and their advantages is crucial to making wise choices.

Investigate insurance companies that provide coverage specific to personal care and cosmetics. Seek out insurance with product liability coverage, which offers particular defense against lawsuits about the functionality and safety of products. If you want more protection against hazards associated with your business, think about getting general liability insurance or other coverage choices.

Make sure that the coverage limits, exclusions, and deductible amounts of the insurance policy you choose fit your budget and your company's demands. Find the ideal policy for your milk bath business by working with insurance brokers or agents who specialize in small businesses or cosmetics. They can offer you individualized help. You can feel secure knowing that you have enough liability insurance to guard against unforeseen circumstances and preserve your finances.

CONTROL MEASURES FOR QUALITY: GUARANTEEING PRODUCT RELIABILITY AND SECURITY

Putting quality control procedures in place is essential to guaranteeing the dependability and security of your milk bath goods. In addition to satisfying client expectations, consistent quality fosters loyalty and trust. To begin with, setting up efficient quality control procedures calls for close attention to detail, standardization, and continual performance evaluation of the product.

Begin by drafting comprehensive product specs that specify the qualities you want your milk bath items to have, like texture, strength of scent, and necessary packaging. To ensure the quality and purity of raw materials, thoroughly source and test ingredients. Create production procedures that emphasize precision, cleanliness, and adherence to industry standards.

Check completed items regularly to ensure they meet quality requirements and are consistent and safe. Perform product performance assessments, stability tests, and microbiological tests as part of your quality control processes. Maintain thorough records of all quality control operations, including batch logs, test findings, and remedial measures implemented if deviations arise.

You can show your clients that you are committed to providing them with dependable, safe, and efficient milk bath products by devoting time and resources to quality control. Long-term business success is facilitated by consistent quality, which enhances brand reputation, promotes good evaluations, and repeat business.

MANAGING CLIENT COMPLAINTS: EXPERTLY RESOLVING PROBLEMS

Sustaining client happiness and loyalty requires efficiently managing complaints from customers. Regardless of how successfully you run your milk bath company, problems will inevitably come up from time to time, and how you handle them will affect your reputation. For newcomers, establishing a methodical complaint handling process can transform obstacles into chances for enhancement and client retention.

Establishing unambiguous channels of communication, such as email, phone, or a special customer service portal, is a good place to start for consumers to voice their concerns or provide feedback. Teach your customer care representatives to listen to consumers with empathy, get pertinent details about the problem, and answer in a timely and kind manner. Confirm that complaints have been received and give a deadline for their resolution.

Prioritize the happiness of your customers while handling complaints by providing options such as product replacements, refunds, or savings on subsequent purchases. To track patterns and find opportunities for process or product improvement, keep a record of all encounters and resolves. Make continual improvements to your milk bath goods and customer experience by utilizing feedback from complaints.

In addition to immediately resolving problems, addressing customer complaints with compassion, openness, and dedication to finding a solution enhances rapport with customers and fosters trust. To improve your products and services over time, you should encourage customers to submit candid feedback.

CHAPTER EIGHT

GROWING YOUR COMPANY

GROWTH IN PRODUCTION

Increasing your output is necessary to keep up with the rising demand. To begin, examine your present production procedure to find any bottlenecks and potential areas for enhancement. To effectively raise batch sizes, think about investing in one larger piece of equipment or several smaller ones. Streamline processes to increase productivity and reduce downtime.

Next, assess the procurement of your raw materials to guarantee availability and consistent quality. Strike deals with suppliers for bulk discounts to lower unit costs and increase profit margins. As production increases, put quality control procedures in place to ensure that product standards are met. Review and modify production schedules often to efficiently meet market demands.

OPTIONS FOR OUTSOURCING

Increasing efficiency and concentrating on key competencies can be achieved by strategically outsourcing some work. Determine whether non-core tasks, such as labeling, marketing, or packaging, can be delegated to expert service providers.

Find trustworthy partners with a track record of success and competitive pricing by conducting in-depth research.

To guarantee efficient cooperation and high-quality results, contracts should clearly outline expectations and deliveries. Keep a tight eye on any activities that are outsourced to ensure control and quickly resolve any problems. Make sure your outsourcing partners are still meeting your needs as a business by routinely reviewing their performance.

EMPLOYING SUPPORT STAFF

It becomes increasingly important to hire more team members as your firm expands. Clearly define roles and duties to prevent task duplication and promote effective teamwork. Look for applicants who share the same values and corporate culture as you, along with the necessary expertise and skills.

To ensure a seamless on boarding process for new employees, provide them with sufficient training and support.

Create an atmosphere at work that is supportive of teamwork, creativity, and ongoing education.

Evaluate workforce requirements regularly and change as needed to support business expansion.

INVENTORY CONTROL

Achieving cost-effective inventory management while satisfying consumer demand is essential. Put inventory management systems in place to precisely track reorder points, sales patterns, and stock levels. Sort inventory according to turnover rates to reduce storage expenses and give priority to stocking.

Increase sales by introducing new varieties, combining products, or running promotions to maximize inventory turnover.

To find and fix inconsistencies, cut waste, and enhance inventory accuracy, conduct routine audits.

Make use of forecasting technologies to predict changes in demand and modify inventory levels appropriately.

BUDGETING

Profitability and sustainable expansion depend on sound financial planning. Make a thorough budget that takes into consideration all costs, such as overhead, marketing, production, and any unforeseen circumstances.

Regularly assess progress and pinpoint areas for improvement by analyzing important metrics and keeping an eye on financial performance.

To increase accuracy and streamline financial procedures, spend money on technologies like accounting software. Establish attainable income goals and create plans to reach them, such as broadening your product line or entering new markets. To guarantee proper financial management and regulatory compliance, get experienced counsel from financial specialists.

CHAPTER NINE

CONSUMER INPUT AND ENHANCEMENT

GETTING INPUT

To begin collecting feedback for your milk bath goods, set up many channels where customers may submit reviews. Encourage customers to share their experiences by using your email newsletters, social media accounts, and website. Provide discounts or free samples as rewards to people who submit thorough comments. Additionally, think about utilizing online survey tools to get organized input on particular features of your products, such as preferred packaging, scents, and prices.

Ask open-ended questions that compel clients to go into further detail about their experiences to optimize the quality of their feedback.

For instance, find out what they loved most about the product and whether there is anything that may be improved upon, rather than just asking if they liked it. Keep an eye on internet review sites and reply to reviews—both good and bad—as soon as possible. Interact with clients to convey that you respect their opinions and are dedicated to making ongoing improvements to your products in response to their suggestions.

EXAMINING INPUT

To find common trends and areas for improvement, answers from customers are categorized into themes during the analysis process. To determine the general sentiment of reviews—whether favorable, negative, or neutral—use technologies such as sentiment analysis software.

Pay heed to feedback that keeps coming in about how well a product works, problems with the packaging, your preferred aroma, or worries about the price. Establish a mechanism for monitoring and classifying comments so that nothing is missed.

Sort input into categories and rank the issues that need to be fixed right away vs. those that can wait for further revisions of the product. Think about setting up a feedback loop where you inform clients regularly about the modifications that have been made in response to their input.

Proving that their opinions are respected and taken into consideration, not only demonstrates transparency but also strengthens client loyalty.

ITERATIVE DESIGN

Iterative development is making adjustments to your milk bath goods in response to customer input. Priorities feedback first according to how it affects market demand and consumer happiness. If consumers frequently express a preference for items with more natural ingredients, for instance, you might choose to restructure your product's recipe. Before introducing novel formulations to a wider audience, closely collaborate with your production staff to evaluate and improve them.

Inform your clients of any modifications openly and honestly, emphasizing any advancements made in response to their input. To get input on new features or enhancements before fully incorporating them into your product line, think about releasing limited edition batches. Keep a careful eye on how customers react to iterations and be ready to make additional changes in response to input when it becomes available.

ONGOING INNOVATION

Maintaining a competitive edge in the market and satisfying changing customer demands require constant innovation. By coming up with new features or product concepts that cater to the needs or wants of your target market, you can use client feedback as a spark for innovation. To keep up with new developments in skincare technology and trends, work with industry professionals or carry out market research.

Review your product range regularly and, depending on consumer feedback and market demand, decide which sectors to expand or diversify. Try different product formats, package styles, or fragrances to keep your offers interesting and appealing to a larger market. Utilize client input to direct your innovation strategy and maintain a competitive edge by continuously producing value-added items.

ADDRESSING CRITICISM

Respond to criticism by taking a professional and constructive stance towards unfavorable comments. Recognize the client's worries and extend your regret for any inconvenience they may have caused. Provide remedies or substitutes to make things right, like refunds, exchanges, or savings on subsequent purchases. Refrain from becoming combative or offering justifications, as this may worsen the circumstance.

Take advantage of unfavorable comments to enhance your offerings and customer support procedures. To find any underlying problems that might have added to the unpleasant experience, conduct internal reviews and take prompt action to resolve them. Maintain open lines of communication with disgruntled clients to make sure their issues are appropriately addressed and that they receive a sense of respect and hearing.

CHAPTER TEN

EXTENDING OFFERINGS AND PRODUCT LINE

PRODUCT DIVERSIFICATION: EXPANDING YOUR RANGE BY INCLUDING COMPLIMENTARY ITEMS

By providing a variety of supplementary goods that improve your primary offers, product diversification is a calculated strategy for growing your milk bath business. For instance, you might start using bath salts, essential oil mixtures loofahs, and bath bombs as bathroom accessories.

These goods give clients a full spa experience in addition to enhancing your milk baths. When expanding your product line, take into account the tastes of your intended market and try to close any gaps in the industry that complement the identity of your brand.

Do market research to find popular products and consumer wants so that you may efficiently diversify your product range. To learn more about the requirements and preferences of your current clients, you can also examine their feedback. Make sure the complimentary items you've chosen are of the highest caliber and represent the principles of your business. Create interesting product descriptions and bundle promotions to entice clients to check out different products from your selection. Increasing sales prospects and expanding your consumer base are possible outcomes of providing a varied assortment of products.

SEASONAL VARIATIONS: MAKING SPECIAL OCCASION LIMITED-EDITION MILK BATHS

Creating limited-edition goods for particular seasons or events, such as holidays, festivals, or seasonal shifts, is known as seasonal variants in milk baths. For example, around the holidays you may create milk baths with a winter theme and scents like cinnamon or peppermint. Similar to this, tropically inspired mixtures work well for summertime, while floral-infused milk baths might be wonderful for spring. You may take advantage of seasonal demand and draw in seasonal customers by matching your items with seasonal trends.

If you want to use seasonal changes to good advantage, schedule your product launches according to the seasonal calendar beforehand. To determine popular colors and scents that correspond with each season, conduct market research. Make eye-catching packaging that embodies the concept of every seasonal change to lure customers in with exclusive products.

Make use of email marketing and social media to advertise your seasonal goods, stressing their limited availability and uniqueness. During peak seasons, you can increase sales and generate customer interest by implementing seasonal variations into your product plan.

PARTNERSHIPS & COLLABORATIONS: GAINING ADVANTAGES BY COOPERATING WITH OTHER BRANDS

Your milk bath business can gain a lot from collaborations and partnerships by reaching a wider audience, entering new markets, and utilizing the advantages of other companies. Find possible partners who provide related products or services to your target market. One way to draw clients interested in holistic well-being is to work with a skincare brand to develop a skincare bundle that includes a milk bath. Similarly, collaborating on co-promotion with a nearby spa or wellness center can raise brand awareness and legitimacy.

Reach out to possible partners with a well-written proposal that highlights the benefits of the partnership on both sides to start collaborations and partnerships. To get the most visibility and interaction, work together on collaborative events, marketing initiatives, and product development.

Use each other's resources and networks to expand your reach and draw in new clients. Track the effectiveness of your partnerships and get client input to evaluate the partnership's success. In the industry, you can increase revenue, strengthen your brand, and create enduring relationships by encouraging strategic collaborations.

CUSTOMISATION SERVICES: PROVIDING CLIENTS WITH INDIVIDUALIZED CHOICES

With customization services, you can give your clients individualized alternatives for their milk bath experience, meeting their specific needs and preferences. Give customers the ability to customize their order by selecting colors, smells, and extras (such as dried flowers or herbs) as well as package designs. For an additional personalized touch, think about providing personalized labels or gift wrapping. Personalization increases client pleasure and encourages word-of-mouth recommendations and loyalty.

Provide a simple way for clients to choose their preferences during the ordering process to successfully implement customization services. To provide a seamless and user-friendly experience, provide clients with clear and simple instructions that walk them through the customization possibilities. To make the customization process easier, make use of technology, such as online forms or tools for website customization. Maintain regular contact with clients to find out their preferences and handle any unique requests or issues. You can set your business apart from the competition, provide consumers with experiences they won't soon forget, and improve client retention by providing personalized options.

SUSTAINABILITY INITIATIVES: INCLUDING ENVIRONMENTALLY FRIENDLY PROCEDURES IN YOUR OPERATIONS

To attract eco-aware customers and show a dedication to environmental responsibility, modern businesses—including those in the milk bath industry—must implement sustainability programs. Include environmentally beneficial activities like recycling programs, utilizing biodegradable packaging, obtaining organic and responsibly farmed ingredients, and reducing water consumption. Inform clients about your sustainability initiatives clearly and concisely, emphasizing the advantages of your operations and products for the environment.

Set quantifiable sustainability targets and carry out an environmental audit of your company to find areas for improvement to successfully integrate sustainability activities. Obtain products and ingredients from reliable vendors who follow sustainable practices or have earned eco-certifications. Inform your clientele of the harm that traditional bath products do to the environment and the advantages of selecting eco-friendly substitutes, such as your milk baths.

CHAPTER ELEVEN

PROSPECTS & TRENDS FOR THE FUTURE

SECTORAL PATTERNS

Keeping up with market trends is essential for every business, even those who sell milk bath products. The growing desire for natural and organic ingredients is one trend to watch. Natural milk bath products are a popular choice since consumers are becoming more and more drawn to goods that are free from harsh chemicals and unnatural additives. The emphasis on environmental friendliness and sustainability is another trend. A devoted customer base can be attracted by providing eco-friendly packaging and sustainable production methods since consumers are becoming more aware of the environmental impact of their purchases.

Additionally, customization—including milk baths—is becoming more popular in the wellness and cosmetic sectors. Providing individualized choices for scents, packaging alternatives, and additives like essential oils or flower petals can improve client satisfaction and distinguish your business. In addition, milk baths might be positioned as a calming and revitalizing component of a self-care ritual, as self-care and wellness routines are becoming more popular.

DEVELOPING MARKETS

Investigating emerging markets may provide the milk bath industry with fresh growth prospects. Targeting particular demographics—like Gen Z and millennials, who value natural products and self-care—is an important thing to think about.

Since these younger customers are frequently engaged on social media, influencer partnerships, and digital marketing techniques are useful in connecting with them.

Geographically, it can be advantageous to enter regions where there is a rising demand for health and cosmetics items. These can include communities with a significant spa culture, popular vacation spots with a focus on health, or places where demand for natural skincare products is rising. You may expand your consumer base and boost sales prospects by locating and entering these developing areas.

INTEGRATION OF TECHNOLOGY

Using technology in your milk bath business can improve client experiences and expedite processes.

Reaching a larger audience than just your local market is possible when you use e-commerce platforms for online sales. By putting customer relationship management (CRM) systems into place, businesses may better manage their customers' preferences, data, and feedback, which allows for more individualized marketing efforts and increased customer retention.

Additionally, increasing brand visibility and engagement can be achieved by utilizing digital marketing tools and social media. Developing interesting content—like how-to guides for milk baths, client endorsements, and targeted advertising—will draw in new clients and establish the brand's legitimacy. Adopting technology makes your company more efficient and presents it as cutting-edge and customer-focused.

INITIATIVES FOR EDUCATION

In the milk bath business, educational programs are essential to establishing consumer trust and brand authority. Organizing talks and demonstrations about subjects like the health advantages of milk baths, how to make homemade versions at home, and skincare advice will draw in new clients and inform existing ones about your offerings. Creating instructive content in collaboration with beauty and wellness influencers or professionals can further strengthen its reputation.

Additionally, providing educational guides or blog entries on your website about subjects like product safety, ingredient sourcing, and skincare practices present your company as informed and reliable.

Providing clients with informative content not only assists them in making well-informed purchases but also cultivates advocacy and loyalty.

WORLDWIDE GROWTH

There are many exciting prospects for business growth and market penetration when you take your milk bath company global. Your expansion strategy might be guided by carrying out market research to discover target foreign markets that need natural skin care products and are prepared to pay for high-end quality. Achieving success in global expansion requires a thorough understanding of cultural preferences, regulations, and distribution methods in various regions.

A smooth introduction into foreign markets is ensured by working with area distributors or retailers, modifying product labeling and packaging to meet local regulations, and streamlining shipping operations. International customer acquisition and retention can be facilitated by utilizing digital channels for global marketing campaigns and localization tactics, such as translating product details and website content into target languages. Expanding internationally not only boosts income possibilities but also fortifies your brand's position in the cutthroat beauty and wellness sector.

Made in United States
Troutdale, OR
09/23/2024

23058968R00056